This Book Belongs to _____

Introduction

The basic skill a kid needs to become a Scientist , Engineer , Astronaut or a successful businessman is MATH.

The Daily Math Practice Workbook Pre-Algebra for Grades 7-8 includes essentials Math skills for K-12 . These worksheets are reproducible and ready to use in classrooms as well as in homes . The Daily Practice of math builds essentials math skills that will be used in later math concepts/ Topics. These worksheets are fun to complete within 5 to 20 minutes. After completing this book, the students will be able to recognize, understand and solve the problems of these topics and provide best possible solution . This book will help students build problem solving and decision making skills.

Moreover , **the teachers as well as parents can assess the kids.** Yes! Each worksheet can be graded , so you can track the progress of the students daily . You have the opportunity to decide your own scoring mechanism, i.e. 10/10, 20/20.

Finally, **the solution for each worksheet is provided in the back of the book** to verify the answers or check if the students are on right path to solving the problem.

This book is the **perfect combination of fun and math**. We hope that all students enjoy this book and build required math skills for bright future.

Table of Contents

Order of Operations (PEDMAS)
Find the solution.

1. $75 + 67 - 72 =$ _____

2. $30 + 48 - 92 =$ _____

3. $46 + 26^2 =$ _____

4. $29 + 9^2 =$ _____

5. $(32 + 65)(79 - 55) =$ _____

6. $93 + (13 \times 47) =$ _____

7. $69 + 87^2 + 72 + 10^2 =$ _____

8. $43 + (-44) + (-96) =$ _____

9. $(36 + 40)^2 =$ _____

10. $25 + 38^2 =$ _____

Order of Operations (PEDMAS)
Find the solution.

① $42 + 9 + 31 =$ _____

② $96 + (80 + 70) =$ _____

③ $8 \times (58 + 18) =$ _____

④ $(2^2) \times (49^2) + 57 =$ _____

⑤ $(89^2) \times (90^2) + 47 =$ _____

⑥ $29 \times (75 + 1) =$ _____

⑦ $3 + (-15) + 73 =$ _____

⑧ $(25 + 4)^2 + (59 + 89)^2 =$ _____

⑨ $94 + 91 + 2 + 5 =$ _____

⑩ $(23 + 58) \div 33 =$ _____

Order of Operations (PEDMAS)
Find the solution.

①　$17 + (-13) + 10 =$ _____

②　$70 - 95 - (-44) =$ _____

③　$(3 + 48)^2 + (59 + 16)^2 =$ _____

④　$(-71) - 15 - 93 =$ _____

⑤　$18 \times 5 \times 71 =$ _____

⑥　$8 \times 86 \times 79 =$ _____

⑦　$6 - 53 - (-94) =$ _____

⑧　$43 \times 17 =$ _____

⑨　$40(67 + 16) =$ _____

⑩　$43 \times 82 =$ _____

Order of Operations (PEDMAS)
Find the solution.

(1) $47 + (99 \times 57) =$ _____

(2) $64 + (43 \times 61) =$ _____

(3) $2 \times (30 + 57) =$ _____

(4) $99 \times 75 + 68 =$ _____

(5) $16 \times 88 + 47 =$ _____

(6) $(-86) + (-23) + 70 =$ _____

(7) $(92 + 30)(29 - 28) =$ _____

(8) $(60^2) \times (66^2) + 59 =$ _____

(9) $17 + (-37) + 54 =$ _____

(10) $(60 + 10)15 - 22 =$ _____

Order of Operations (PEDMAS)
Find the solution.

① $59 \times (44 - 7) =$ _____

② $31 \times (83 - 46) =$ _____

③ $15 + 46 - 84 + 21 =$ _____

④ $(-58) - 89 - (-70) =$ _____

⑤ $20 + 39(91 + 5) =$ _____

⑥ $26 + 25 + 48 =$ _____

⑦ $69 + (-47 + 84) =$ _____

⑧ $54 + 80 + 28 =$ _____

⑨ $(57 \times 40) - (90 + 92) =$ _____

⑩ $(70 + 36) \div 91 =$ _____

Order of Operations (PEDMAS)
Find the solution.

① $(93 + 63)(99 - 18) =$ _____

② $13 \times 67 =$ _____

③ $5 + (-25) + 74 =$ _____

④ $32 + 90 - 69 + 13 =$ _____

⑤ $59 + 52 + 51 =$ _____

⑥ $55 \times 89 + 74 =$ _____

⑦ $55 \times (91 + 51) =$ _____

⑧ $(22 \times 97) - (79 + 51) =$ _____

⑨ $23 - (-32) - (-77) =$ _____

⑩ $(-92) + 35 + 9 =$ _____

Order of Operations (PEDMAS)
Find the solution.

① $95 + 5 + 1 =$ _____

② $22 - 56 - (-57) =$ _____

③ $(8 + 77)(78 - 1) =$ _____

④ $(64 + 59)(34 - 43) =$ _____

⑤ $42(2 + 38) =$ _____

⑥ $(-62) - 45 + (-72) =$ _____

⑦ $48 + 82^2 + 96 + 81^2 =$ _____

⑧ $14 + 91^2 + 67 + 61^2 =$ _____

⑨ $70 + (45 - 45) =$ _____

⑩ $3 \times 69 =$ _____

Order of Operations (PEDMAS)
Find the solution.

1. $(-34) + 45 + 96 =$ _____

2. $87 + 48 + 48 =$ _____

3. $79 + (-72) + 82 =$ _____

4. $(28 + 14)19 - 14 =$ _____

5. $9 + 20 + 8 + 65 =$ _____

6. $90 + 46 - (8 + 33) =$ _____

7. $(55 + 62) \div 89 =$ _____

8. $(-10) + 87 + 26 =$ _____

9. $4 + (80 \times 67) =$ _____

10. $79 - (-48) - (-49) =$ _____

Order of Operations (PEDMAS)
Find the solution.

(1) $74 \times 56 =$ _____

(2) $6 \times (42 + 8) =$ _____

(3) $(78 + 50) \div 30 =$ _____

(4) $75 + (-78) - 92 =$ _____

(5) $(-81) - 79 - 82 =$ _____

(6) $7 + (-78) + 61 =$ _____

(7) $23 + (-75) - (-91) =$ _____

(8) $(15 + 48)(66 - 70) =$ _____

(9) $46 + 46^2 + 82 + 90^2 =$ _____

(10) $61 \times (71 + 33) =$ _____

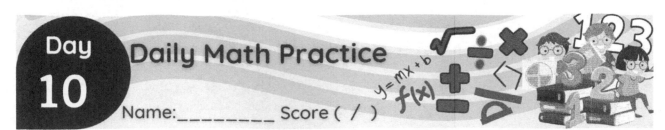

Order of Operations (PEDMAS)
Find the solution.

1. $38 + (-4) - 69 =$ _____

2. $57 + 87 - 83 + 54 =$ _____

3. $11(-25 + 58) =$ _____

4. $90 \times (15 - 81) =$ _____

5. $48 \times 27 + 90 =$ _____

6. $(-35) - 96 - 62 =$ _____

7. $(95 + 60)^2 + (68 + 5)^2 =$ _____

8. $45 + (-75) - 21 =$ _____

9. $(-86) + 95 - 73 =$ _____

10. $74 + 16 + 5 =$ _____

Lowest Common Multiple
Find the lowest common multiple.

1) 10
   6
   _____ ____

2) 12
   10
   _____ ____

3) 3
   11
   _____ ____

4) 10
   8
   _____ ____

5) 10
   9
   _____ ____

6) 7
   12
   _____ ____

7) 11
   9
   _____ ____

8) 11
   7
   _____ ____

Lowest Common Multiple

Find the lowest common multiple.

① 10
   11 _____ ___

② 11
   10 _____ ___

③ 2
   10 _____ ___

④ 11
   12 _____ ___

⑤ 7
   9 _____ ___

⑥ 3
   8 _____ ___

⑦ 5
   12 _____ ___

⑧ 4
   11 _____ ___

Lowest Common Multiple
Find the lowest common multiple.

1) 2
    9

2) 12
    11

3) 12
    2

4) 2
    10

5) 10
    2

6) 11
    8

7) 10
    4

8) 10
    12

Lowest Common Multiple

Find the lowest common multiple.

1) 3
    7 _____ ____

2) 9
    12 _____ ____

3) 10
    11 _____ ____

4) 2
    5 _____ ____

5) 12
    10 _____ ____

6) 12
    5 _____ ____

7) 11
    7 _____ ____

8) 6
    12 _____ ____

Lowest Common Multiple
Find the lowest common multiple.

1. 10
   4
   _____ ___

2. 10
   12
   _____ ___

3. 7
   5
   _____ ___

4. 12
   11
   _____ ___

5. 12
   10
   _____ ___

6. 7
   3
   _____ ___

7. 7
   12
   _____ ___

8. 10
   3
   _____ ___

Lowest Common Multiple
Find the lowest common multiple.

1) 10
   8 _____

2) 2
   7 _____

3) 11
   12 _____

4) 5
   10 _____

5) 8
   4 _____

6) 9
   3 _____

7) 2
   11 _____

8) 9
   12 _____

Lowest Common Multiple
Find the lowest common multiple.

1. 8
   3 _____ ____

2. 12
   11 _____ ____

3. 10
   3 _____ ____

4. 10
   12 _____ ____

5. 6
   11 _____ ____

6. 10
   6 _____ ____

7. 5
   2 _____ ____

8. 6
   9 _____ ____

Lowest Common Multiple
Find the lowest common multiple.

1. 12
   11 _____ _____

2. 11
   10 _____ _____

3. 5
   10 _____ _____

4. 2
   5 _____ _____

5. 9
   12 _____ _____

6. 11
   3 _____ _____

7. 12
   10 _____ _____

8. 7
   11 _____ _____

Lowest Common Multiple
Find the lowest common multiple.

(1) 11
    3 _____ ____

(2) 4
    6 _____ ____

(3) 8
    10 _____ ____

(4) 8
    11 _____ ____

(5) 11
    2 _____ ____

(6) 12
    6 _____ ____

(7) 11
    7 _____ ____

(8) 12
    10 _____ ____

Lowest Common Multiple
Find the lowest common multiple.

① 6
   11 _____ ___

② 7
   2 _____ ___

③ 11
   10 _____ ___

④ 3
   9 _____ ___

⑤ 7
   4 _____ ___

⑥ 9
   12 _____ ___

⑦ 8
   3 _____ ___

⑧ 12
   5 _____ ___

Daily Math Practice

Name:_____ Score (/)

Fractions: Multiple Operations
Find the solution.

1. $\dfrac{2}{3} \times \dfrac{3}{5} \times \dfrac{1}{6} =$

2. $\left(\dfrac{1}{4} + \dfrac{1}{5}\right) \div \dfrac{1}{3} =$

3. $\dfrac{1}{4} + \dfrac{5}{6} + 9 =$

4. $\dfrac{1}{3} + \dfrac{1}{6} + \dfrac{4}{5} + \dfrac{1}{6} =$

5. $\dfrac{5}{6} \times \dfrac{2}{5} + \dfrac{2}{5} =$

Fractions: Multiple Operations

Find the solution.

1. $\left(\dfrac{1}{3} + \dfrac{3}{8}\right) - \left(\dfrac{2}{3} \times \dfrac{1}{6}\right) =$

2. $\dfrac{3}{4} \times \dfrac{1}{4} \times \dfrac{2}{3} =$

3. $\left(\dfrac{1}{6} \times \dfrac{1}{3}\right) + \left(\dfrac{1}{4} \times \dfrac{1}{3}\right) =$

4. $\left(\dfrac{1}{6} + \dfrac{1}{3}\right) - \left(\dfrac{5}{8} \times \dfrac{7}{8}\right) =$

5. $\left(\dfrac{5}{8} + \dfrac{3}{5}\right) \div \dfrac{1}{5} =$

Fractions: Multiple Operations

Find the solution.

① $\dfrac{2}{3} + \dfrac{2}{3} + \dfrac{3}{4} + \dfrac{1}{4} =$

② $\dfrac{1}{4} \times \dfrac{5}{8} + \dfrac{1}{4} =$

③ $\dfrac{1}{4} \times \dfrac{1}{3} \times \dfrac{2}{3} =$

④ $\dfrac{1}{4} + \dfrac{1}{6} - \dfrac{1}{4} =$

⑤ $\left(\dfrac{1}{3} \times \dfrac{1}{4}\right) + \left(\dfrac{3}{8} \times \dfrac{3}{4}\right) =$

Fractions: Multiple Operations

Find the solution.

1. $\dfrac{1}{3} + \dfrac{1}{8} + 3 =$

2. $\dfrac{1}{4} + \dfrac{1}{3} + \dfrac{1}{4} + \dfrac{1}{6} =$

3. $\left(\dfrac{5}{8} + \dfrac{2}{3}\right) - \left(\dfrac{1}{8} \times \dfrac{2}{3}\right) =$

4. $\dfrac{1}{4} + \dfrac{1}{4} + \dfrac{1}{4} =$

5. $\left(\dfrac{1}{5} \times \dfrac{1}{6}\right) + \left(\dfrac{1}{6} \times \dfrac{1}{5}\right) =$

Fractions: Multiple Operations

Find the solution.

① $\left(\dfrac{5}{8} + \dfrac{3}{4}\right) - \left(\dfrac{5}{8} \times \dfrac{5}{8}\right) =$

② $\dfrac{5}{6} \times \dfrac{4}{5} \times \dfrac{1}{3} =$

③ $\left(\dfrac{1}{5} + \dfrac{1}{4}\right) - \left(\dfrac{3}{8} \times \dfrac{2}{3}\right) =$

④ $\dfrac{4}{5} \times \dfrac{1}{3} \times \dfrac{2}{3} =$

⑤ $\left(\dfrac{1}{3} + \dfrac{1}{6}\right) - \left(\dfrac{1}{4} \times \dfrac{2}{3}\right) =$

Fractions: Multiple Operations

Find the solution.

(1) $\dfrac{1}{4} \times \dfrac{3}{4} + \dfrac{2}{3} =$

(2) $\dfrac{1}{6} + \dfrac{3}{4} + 8 =$

(3) $\left(\dfrac{2}{3} \times \dfrac{2}{3}\right) + \left(\dfrac{1}{6} \times \dfrac{7}{8}\right) =$

(4) $\dfrac{1}{5} \times \dfrac{1}{4} \times \dfrac{2}{3} =$

(5) $\left(\dfrac{3}{4} + \dfrac{2}{5}\right) \div \dfrac{1}{3} =$

Daily Math Practice

Name:_____ Score (/)

Fractions: Multiple Operations
Find the solution.

1. $\dfrac{3}{8} + \dfrac{1}{6} - \dfrac{1}{4} =$

2. $\left(\dfrac{1}{6} + \dfrac{1}{8}\right) \times \left(\dfrac{1}{3} + \dfrac{1}{3}\right) =$

3. $\dfrac{1}{3} \times \dfrac{1}{3} \times \dfrac{2}{5} =$

4. $\left(\dfrac{1}{4} + \dfrac{1}{6}\right) \div \dfrac{4}{5} =$

5. $\dfrac{1}{4} \times \dfrac{3}{8} + \dfrac{2}{3} =$

Fractions: Multiple Operations

Find the solution.

1. $\dfrac{1}{4} + \dfrac{1}{6} + 9 =$

2. $\dfrac{2}{5} \times \dfrac{2}{5} + \dfrac{2}{3} =$

3. $\left(\dfrac{4}{5} + \dfrac{1}{4}\right) - \left(\dfrac{5}{6} \times \dfrac{1}{3}\right) =$

4. $\left(\dfrac{1}{3} + \dfrac{1}{4}\right) \times \left(\dfrac{5}{6} + \dfrac{3}{5}\right) =$

5. $\dfrac{1}{3} \times \dfrac{1}{3} \times \dfrac{1}{3} =$

Fractions: Multiple Operations
Find the solution.

(1) $\dfrac{1}{6} + \dfrac{1}{3} - \dfrac{2}{5} =$

(2) $\left(\dfrac{5}{8} \times \dfrac{3}{4}\right) + \left(\dfrac{1}{4} \times \dfrac{5}{8}\right) =$

(3) $\left(\dfrac{1}{4} + \dfrac{3}{5}\right) \times \left(\dfrac{2}{3} + \dfrac{1}{6}\right) =$

(4) $\left(\dfrac{1}{5} + \dfrac{2}{3}\right) \div \dfrac{3}{4} =$

(5) $\dfrac{3}{5} + \dfrac{1}{3} - \dfrac{3}{5} =$

Fractions: Multiple Operations
Find the solution.

1. $\dfrac{5}{6} + \dfrac{1}{4} + 8 =$

2. $\dfrac{7}{8} + \dfrac{3}{5} + \dfrac{3}{5} =$

3. $\dfrac{1}{6} \times \dfrac{1}{5} \times \dfrac{4}{5} =$

4. $\left(\dfrac{1}{6} + \dfrac{2}{5}\right) \times \left(\dfrac{1}{6} + \dfrac{1}{4}\right) =$

5. $\dfrac{1}{6} + \dfrac{5}{6} + 4 =$

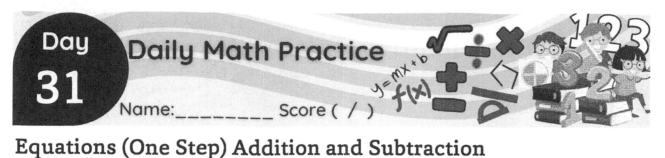
Equations (One Step) Addition and Subtraction
Solve for the variable.

(1) $7x - 4 = 52$

(2) $7x + 1 = 57$

(3) $56 - 6x = 2$

(4) $9 + x = 17$

(5) $x - 1 = 8$

(6) $7 + x = 16$

(7) $2 - x = 0$

(8) $6 - x = 3$

(9) $x + 3 = 8$

(10) $3 + 6x = 57$

Equations (One Step) Addition and Subtraction

Solve for the variable.

(1) $5 + x = 12$

(2) $4x + 3 = 27$

(3) $x + 9 = 14$

(4) $5 - x = 1$

(5) $7x + 4 = 60$

(6) $38 - 6x = 2$

(7) $9 - x = 3$

(8) $7x + 5 = 26$

(9) $4 + x = 8$

(10) $9 - x = 7$

Equations (One Step) Addition and Subtraction
Solve for the variable.

1. $7 - x = 3$

2. $23 - 2x = 7$

3. $9 + 9x = 36$

4. $x - 6 = 1$

5. $1x + 5 = 6$

6. $x + 3 = 7$

7. $52 - 9x = 7$

8. $9 - x = 2$

9. $7 - x = 2$

10. $1x + 3 = 10$

Equations (One Step) Addition and Subtraction
Solve for the variable.

(1) 5 - x = 4

(2) 25 - 8x = 1

(3) 9x + 6 = 69

(4) 7 + 8x = 79

(5) 5 + x = 14

(6) 9x - 1 = 71

(7) 25 - 4x = 5

(8) 9x - 4 = 59

(9) x - 8 = 1

(10) x + 4 = 13

Equations (One Step) Addition and Subtraction

Solve for the variable.

1. $6x + 9 = 27$

2. $8x + 2 = 74$

3. $8 + x = 16$

4. $9 - x = 6$

5. $x - 3 = 3$

6. $1 - x = 0$

7. $48 - 5x = 3$

8. $6 + 7x = 41$

9. $3 + 9x = 66$

10. $7x - 4 = 31$

Equations (One Step) Addition and Subtraction

Solve for the variable.

(1) $x + 7 = 10$

(2) $8 - x = 5$

(3) $x - 2 = 3$

(4) $6 - 1x = 2$

(5) $15 - 1x = 9$

(6) $65 - 9x = 2$

(7) $9x + 6 = 87$

(8) $7x + 2 = 9$

(9) $7x + 4 = 32$

(10) $4x + 3 = 23$

Equations (One Step) Addition and Subtraction
Solve for the variable.

(1) $7 - x = 4$

(2) $4x + 6 = 42$

(3) $8x - 2 = 22$

(4) $7 + x = 11$

(5) $6x + 1 = 19$

(6) $23 - 2x = 5$

(7) $x - 1 = 5$

(8) $7 + 4x = 39$

(9) $x + 2 = 3$

(10) $x - 1 = 6$

Equations (One Step) Addition and Subtraction

Solve for the variable.

1. $6x - 6 = 18$

2. $8 + x = 13$

3. $9 + x = 12$

4. $7x - 1 = 34$

5. $2 + 4x = 6$

6. $x - 5 = 1$

7. $x + 7 = 15$

8. $3 - x = 1$

9. $x + 1 = 7$

10. $3x + 5 = 32$

Equations (One Step) Addition and Subtraction
Solve for the variable.

(1) $9x - 4 = 59$

(2) $7x + 1 = 8$

(3) $24 - 2x = 6$

(4) $2x + 7 = 21$

(5) $x - 4 = 3$

(6) $7x + 8 = 22$

(7) $x + 4 = 8$

(8) $2x + 8 = 14$

(9) $x + 9 = 14$

(10) $6x + 2 = 44$

Daily Math Practice

Name:_____ Score (/)

Equations (One Step) Addition and Subtraction
Solve for the variable.

1. $3x + 8 = 20$

2. $18 - 9x = 0$

3. $9 - x = 3$

4. $8x + 7 = 23$

5. $4 - x = 2$

6. $9 - x = 2$

7. $6 + 6x = 60$

8. $36 - 5x = 6$

9. $x - 3 = 6$

10. $8x - 5 = 11$

Equations (One Step) Multiplication and Division
Solve for the variable.

1. $36 \div x = 4$

2. $4x - 2 = 26$

3. $6x - 5 = 43$

4. $6x + 9 = 27$

5. $x \div 3 = 1$

6. $9 \div x = 9$

7. $x \div 7 = 8$

8. $6x + 7 = 61$

9. $16 - 2x = 6$

10. $8 \times x = 56$

Equations (One Step) Multiplication and Division
Solve for the variable.

(1) $40 \div x = 5$

(2) $x \div 1 = 9$

(3) $1 + 5x = 26$

(4) $6 + 6x = 12$

(5) $x \div 9 = 1$

(6) $x \div 4 = 5$

(7) $19 - 6x = 1$

(8) $8 \times x = 40$

(9) $1x - 5 = 0$

(10) $2x + 2 = 18$

Equations (One Step) Multiplication and Division

Solve for the variable.

(1) $x \times 3 = 18$

(2) $x \div 8 = 9$

(3) $4x - 1 = 31$

(4) $42 \div x = 7$

(5) $9x + 2 = 20$

(6) $18 - 9x = 9$

(7) $31 - 5x = 6$

(8) $13 - 5x = 3$

(9) $5 \times x = 20$

(10) $16 \div x = 4$

Equations (One Step) Multiplication and Division
Solve for the variable.

1. $2x - 6 = 4$

2. $16 - 6x = 4$

3. $5x + 9 = 24$

4. $6 + 3x = 33$

5. $17 - 5x = 2$

6. $4x - 2 = 26$

7. $18 - 3x = 3$

8. $16 - 5x = 1$

9. $52 - 8x = 4$

10. $45 - 5x = 5$

Equations (One Step) Multiplication and Division

Solve for the variable.

1. $8 + 2x = 26$

2. $x \times 1 = 1$

3. $8 \div x = 1$

4. $1 + 4x = 13$

5. $7 \times x = 14$

6. $2x + 3 = 11$

7. $x \div 2 = 4$

8. $x \times 5 = 15$

9. $x \times 9 = 81$

10. $8 + 5x = 48$

Equations (One Step) Multiplication and Division
Solve for the variable.

1. $46 - 5x = 1$

2. $3 \times x = 15$

3. $x \div 3 = 7$

4. $x \times 5 = 35$

5. $6 + 8x = 22$

6. $64 - 7x = 1$

7. $5 + 6x = 59$

8. $9 \times x = 63$

9. $45 \div x = 9$

10. $5x - 8 = 32$

Daily Math Practice

Equations (One Step) Multiplication and Division
Solve for the variable.

(1) $3x + 4 = 22$

(2) $39 - 9x = 3$

(3) $x \div 4 = 3$

(4) $x \div 5 = 8$

(5) $7 - 4x = 3$

(6) $31 - 4x = 7$

(7) $11 - 1x = 2$

(8) $8 + 4x = 40$

(9) $17 - 4x = 1$

(10) $x \div 8 = 1$

Equations (One Step) Multiplication and Division

Solve for the variable.

1. $41 - 7x = 6$

2. $6 + 2x = 22$

3. $x \times 8 = 8$

4. $x \times 3 = 15$

5. $4x + 3 = 7$

6. $x \div 1 = 7$

7. $27 \div x = 9$

8. $x \div 8 = 5$

9. $8x - 5 = 67$

10. $7x - 2 = 5$

Equations (One Step) Multiplication and Division
Solve for the variable.

1. $x \times 2 = 2$

2. $9x - 8 = 28$

3. $7 + 6x = 25$

4. $20 \div x = 5$

5. $x \times 9 = 27$

6. $18 \div x = 6$

7. $33 - 5x = 3$

8. $x \div 2 = 4$

9. $2x + 3 = 13$

10. $x \times 9 = 45$

Equations (One Step) Multiplication and Division
Solve for the variable.

(1) $7 \times x = 63$

(2) $8x - 7 = 17$

(3) $25 - 5x = 5$

(4) $2 \div x = 2$

(5) $2 + 2x = 10$

(6) $2 \times x = 4$

(7) $5x - 8 = 12$

(8) $7x - 1 = 41$

(9) $43 - 7x = 1$

(10) $9 \times x = 36$

Inequalities - Addition and Subtraction
Solve.

1 $x - 4 > 9$

2 $x + 1 > 8$

3 $x + 5 > 2$

4 $3 \leq 2 - x$

5 $7 \leq 5 + x$

6 $9 > 5 - x$

Inequalities - Addition and Subtraction
Solve.

① $9 + x \leq 8$

② $8 \leq x - 7$

③ $8 > x + 8$

④ $7 \leq 5 - x$

⑤ $3 < 6 + x$

⑥ $1 - x < 9$

Daily Math Practice

Name:_____ Score (/)

Inequalities - Addition and Subtraction

Solve.

1. $1 \geq x + 4$

2. $x - 5 \leq 6$

3. $3 - x < 5$

4. $9 + x > 9$

5. $1 < 3 + x$

6. $5 \leq x - 1$

Inequalities - Addition and Subtraction
Solve.

1
$$2 - x \leq 6$$

2
$$x + 1 < 8$$

3
$$8 < x - 2$$

4
$$6 + x \leq 8$$

5
$$x + 6 \leq 6$$

6
$$x - 7 < 9$$

Day 55

Daily Math Practice

Name:_____ Score (/)

Inequalities - Addition and Subtraction
Solve.

1 $6 \geq x + 3$

2 $x - 3 \leq 4$

3 $9 < x + 6$

4 $6 - x \leq 8$

5 $4 < 3 - x$

6 $x + 9 \leq 6$

Inequalities - Addition and Subtraction
Solve.

1. $x + 6 < 8$

2. $x - 7 > 8$

3. $x + 9 > 3$

4. $9 \leq 8 - x$

5. $x - 5 < 6$

6. $4 + x > 2$

Daily Math Practice

Name:_____ Score (/)

Inequalities - Addition and Subtraction
Solve.

1
$$x - 7 > 8$$

2
$$7 + x > 2$$

3
$$8 - x \leq 9$$

4
$$8 \geq x + 2$$

5
$$8 \geq x - 1$$

6
$$4 + x > 5$$

Inequalities - Addition and Subtraction
Solve.

1. $x + 2 > 7$

2. $4 > 1 - x$

3. $x - 8 > 9$

4. $8 + x < 5$

5. $7 > 7 + x$

6. $2 - x < 8$

Daily Math Practice

Inequalities - Addition and Subtraction
Solve.

1 $9 > 4 - x$

2 $x + 3 \leq 7$

3 $x - 8 \geq 9$

4 $6 > x + 1$

5 $4 \geq 9 + x$

6 $6 \geq 3 - x$

Inequalities - Addition and Subtraction
Solve.

1 $2 - x > 6$

2 $7 \leq 6 + x$

3 $x - 7 < 8$

4 $2 \geq x + 9$

5 $3 + x < 6$

6 $5 - x \geq 8$

Daily Math Practice

Name:_____ Score (/)

Inequalities - Multiplication and Division
Solve.

1. $\frac{x}{4} \leq 7$

2. $4 < 8x$

3. $6x > 9$

4. $7 \leq \frac{x}{7}$

5. $12x \geq 18$

6. $8 < \frac{x}{3}$

Daily Math Practice

Name:_____ Score (/)

Inequalities - Multiplication and Division
Solve.

1. $4 \leq 3x$

2. $\frac{x}{2} > 5$

3. $\frac{x}{1} > 1$

4. $12 < 18x$

5. $\frac{x}{4} \leq 7$

6. $4x > 8$

Daily Math Practice

Inequalities - Multiplication and Division
Solve.

1 $\frac{x}{8} > 1$

2 $5 \geq 2x$

3 $1 < \frac{x}{4}$

4 $5 \leq 2x$

5 $12 > 6x$

6 $4 > \frac{x}{3}$

Daily Math Practice

Name:_____ Score (/)

Inequalities - Multiplication and Division
Solve.

1 $\frac{x}{3} \le 8$

2 $9 < 6x$

3 $\frac{x}{8} \ge 8$

4 $4 > 8x$

5 $6 > 5x$

6 $6 \ge \frac{x}{8}$

Inequalities - Multiplication and Division
Solve.

1 $6 < \dfrac{x}{6}$

2 $6\,x < 2$

3 $\dfrac{x}{8} < 5$

4 $2\,x \le 5$

5 $2 \le \dfrac{x}{7}$

6 $12 \ge 8\,x$

Daily Math Practice

Inequalities - Multiplication and Division
Solve.

1 $8x < 12$

2 $\frac{x}{8} \geq 3$

3 $15x > 18$

4 $5 \geq \frac{x}{7}$

5 $18x < 15$

6 $6 > \frac{x}{1}$

Daily Math Practice

Inequalities - Multiplication and Division
Solve.

1 $8 \geq \frac{x}{2}$

2 $12 > 10\,x$

3 $5\,x \geq 6$

4 $2 > \frac{x}{4}$

5 $\frac{x}{3} \geq 4$

6 $6\,x \leq 12$

Inequalities - Multiplication and Division
Solve.

1. $8 > 10x$

2. $\frac{x}{8} \leq 3$

3. $7 \geq \frac{x}{6}$

4. $2x < 5$

5. $9 \geq 12x$

6. $\frac{x}{3} \geq 4$

Inequalities - Multiplication and Division
Solve.

1. $12 \leq 18\,x$

2. $1 > \dfrac{x}{6}$

3. $15\,x > 18$

4. $1 < \dfrac{x}{7}$

5. $\dfrac{x}{3} \leq 3$

6. $15 < 9\,x$

Daily Math Practice

Inequalities - Multiplication and Division
Solve.

1. $8 \geq 4x$

2. $6 \leq \dfrac{x}{6}$

3. $\dfrac{x}{2} > 2$

4. $4 < 4x$

5. $6 < 4x$

6. $5 < \dfrac{x}{5}$

Pre-Algebra Equations (Two Sides)
Solve for the variable.

(1) $8 + 6x + 3 = 31 + x$

(2) $3x = 12 + x$

(3) $15 + x = 3 + 2x + 7$

(4) $86 - 6x = 2 + 8x$

(5) $9x + 6 = 20 + 7x$

(6) $14 + 6x = 9x + 2$

(7) $7x + 2 = 66 - x$

(8) $7x = 30 + x$

(9) $9 + 5x = 45 - x$

(10) $4 + 8x = 94 - 7x$

Pre-Algebra Equations (Two Sides)
Solve for the variable.

1. $7 + x = 4 + 2x$

2. $22 - x + 11 = 7 + 5x + 8$

3. $14 - x = 6 + 2x + 2$

4. $3x = 16 + x$

5. $35 - x = 2 + 2x + 6$

6. $3x + 45 = 9x + 9$

7. $6x + 9 = 25 - 2x$

8. $5x = 20 + x$

9. $26 + x + -3 = 6 + 4x + 2$

10. $5x = 12 + x$

Daily Math Practice

Name:_____ Score (/)

Pre-Algebra Equations (Two Sides)
Solve for the variable.

1. 2 + 4x + 9 = 37 + x + -5

2. 42 - x = 5 + 7x + 5

3. 9 + 2x + 3 = 39 - x

4. 31 - x = 7 + 8x + 6

5. 58 - x = 6 + 8x + 7

6. 34 + x = 6x + 9

7. 9 + 8x = 37 - 6x

8. 6x = 20 + x

9. 42 + x = 7x

10. 10 + 8x = 7 + 9x

Pre-Algebra Equations (Two Sides)

Solve for the variable.

(1) $2x = 5 + x$

(2) $5x + 9 = 37 - 2x$

(3) $3x = 14 + x$

(4) $2 + 2x + 6 = 29 - x$

(5) $5 + 3x = 13 + x$

(6) $6 + 9x = 5x + 34$

(7) $8x + 4 = 124 - 7x$

(8) $3x + 6 = 2x + 11$

(9) $5x = 54 - x$

(10) $8x + 6 = 90 - 6x$

Pre-Algebra Equations (Two Sides)
Solve for the variable.

(1) $5x + 5 = 77 - 4x$

(2) $8x = 56 + x$

(3) $2 + 2x + 9 = 16 + x$

(4) $8x = 28 + x$

(5) $2x = 15 - x$

(6) $6x = 35 - x$

(7) $7x + 7 = 63 - x$

(8) $7x + 5 = 96 - 6x$

(9) $7x = 48 + x$

(10) $2x + 19 = 4x + 3$

Pre-Algebra Equations (Two Sides)
Solve for the variable.

(1) $27 + x = 6x + 2$

(2) $7 + 9x = 126 - 8x$

(3) $55 - 3x = 7 + 5x$

(4) $6x + 5 = 5x + 9$

(5) $5 + 8x = 7x + 14$

(6) $4x + 8 = 33 - x$

(7) $5x + 9 = 45 - x$

(8) $6 + 3x + 2 = 44 - x$

(9) $35 - x = 6x$

(10) $8 + 3x + 9 = 36 + x + -1$

Pre-Algebra Equations (Two Sides)
Solve for the variable.

1. $9 + 8x = 4 + 9x$

2. $7 + 6x = 27 + x$

3. $6x = 35 + x$

4. $2 + 7x = 32 + x$

5. $5 + 7x = 8x + 3$

6. $27 + x = 5x + 3$

7. $16 - x = 3x$

8. $3x + 6 = 18 - x$

9. $9x + 6 = 20 + 2x$

10. $3x = 8 - x$

Daily Math Practice

Pre-Algebra Equations (Two Sides)

Solve for the variable.

(1) $4x = 35 - x$

(2) $9 - x = 2x$

(3) $41 - x = 6x + 6$

(4) $7 + 5x = 49 - x$

(5) $67 - x = 5 + 6x + 6$

(6) $50 - 6x = 8x + 8$

(7) $19 - x = 3x + 7$

(8) $32 - x = 3x$

(9) $2x = 2 + x$

(10) $16 + x = 4 + 3x$

Pre-Algebra Equations (Two Sides)
Solve for the variable.

(1) $18 + x + -5 = 3 + 2x + 2$

(2) $40 + x = 6x$

(3) $5x = 24 - x$

(4) $9 + 6x = 29 + 2x$

(5) $7x = 24 - x$

(6) $7x = 42 + x$

(7) $40 - 4x = 8x + 4$

(8) $16 + x = 5 + 2x + 6$

(9) $25 + 4x = 7x + 7$

(10) $56 - x = 7x$

Daily Math Practice

Name:_____ Score (/)

Pre-Algebra Equations (Two Sides)
Solve for the variable.

1. $4 + 6x = 53 - x$

2. $7x + 7 = 61 - 2x$

3. $38 + x = 6x + 3$

4. $22 + x = 5x + 6$

5. $5 + 8x + 8 = 45 - x + 13$

6. $54 - x = 6 + 4x + 3$

7. $4x + 21 = 7 + 6x$

8. $21 + x = 9 + 6x + 2$

9. $52 - 2x = 9x + 8$

10. $2x = 8 + x$

Pre-Algebra Equations (Two Sides)
Solve for the variable.

(1)　$29 + x + 1 = 8 + 3x + 8$

(2)　$47 - x + 14 = 5 + 7x + 8$

(3)　$26 - x = 5x + 2$

(4)　$9 + 6x = 3 + 8x$

(5)　$7 + x = 2x$

(6)　$4 + 2x + 9 = 21 + x$

(7)　$35 - x = 5 + 5x$

(8)　$9x + 6 = 125 - 8x$

(9)　$4x = 9 + x$

(10)　$9 + 6x = 6 + 7x$

Pre-Algebra Equations (Two Sides)

Solve for the variable.

1. $82 - 7x = 9x + 2$

2. $25 - x = 3x + 9$

3. $35 + x + 0 = 4 + 8x + 3$

4. $7x + 12 = 9x + 6$

5. $7 + 6x = 42 - x$

6. $17 - x + 14 = 7 + 2x + 3$

7. $15 + x + 7 = 9 + 3x + 9$

8. $4 + 6x = 54 - 4x$

9. $56 - x = 7x$

10. $4 + 2x + 7 = 11 - x + 6$

Pre-Algebra Equations (Two Sides)

Solve for the variable.

1. $8x + 9 = 105 - 4x$

2. $45 - x = 4x$

3. $4x = 45 - x$

4. $35 + x = 8x$

5. $6x = 30 + x$

6. $6 + 8x = 20 + x$

7. $50 - x = 2 + 5x$

8. $31 + x + 4 = 8 + 7x + 3$

9. $35 + x = 6x$

10. $60 - x = 7x + 4$

Pre-Algebra Equations (Two Sides)
Solve for the variable.

(1) $36 - x + 8 = 4 + 8x + 4$

(2) $6x + 22 = 8x + 6$

(3) $51 + x = 7x + 9$

(4) $6 + 3x + 8 = 27 - x + 15$

(5) $12 + x = 7x$

(6) $26 + x = 5 + 5x + 9$

(7) $5x = 24 - x$

(8) $25 - x + 6 = 2 + 4x + 9$

(9) $2x = 27 - x$

(10) $5 + 4x = 11 + x$

Pre-Algebra Equations (Two Sides)
Solve for the variable.

1. $33 + 2x = 8x + 9$

2. $2x = 6 - x$

3. $68 - x = 8x + 5$

4. $24 - 4x = 2 + 7x$

5. $4 + 9x = 72 - 8x$

6. $24 + x + 0 = 9 + 2x + 6$

7. $31 + 3x = 7 + 7x$

8. $9x + 4 = 106 - 8x$

9. $3x + 5 = 25 - x$

10. $23 - x = 5 + 8x$

Simplifying Expressions

1. x + 6 + x

2. 9x - 1 - 4x + 8

3. 6x + 4 + 7x

4. -1 + 5x - x - 7 - 2x

5. -x - 8x

6. -3 + 7x + 1 - 9x

7. -7x + x

Simplifying Expressions

(1) x - 3 + 4x - 5 + 8x + 1

(2) -8x - 4 + 9x

(3) -1 + 3x + 3 - 5x

(4) 5x - 7 - 2x + 9

(5) -6x + 6x + 2 - 2x

(6) -3 + 6x + 3 - 4x

(7) 8x - 8x + 3 + 6

Simplifying Expressions

(1) $9x + 8 + 2x$

(2) $6x - 8x + 6x - 3 + 4$

(3) $6x - 4x$

(4) $8x + 1 + x$

(5) $1 + 5x + 7 + 8x$

(6) $6x - x + 4 + 8$

(7) $1 + 5x - 9 + 8x - 8 + x$

Simplifying Expressions

① $-7x + 6 + 2x + 7 + 8x - 7$

② $-x + 4x$

③ $6 + 7x - 8x + 4 - 4x$

④ $7 + 3x - 8x + 4 - 9x$

⑤ $5 - 1(x - 3)$

⑥ $7 + 9x - 9 + 4x$

⑦ $x + 1 + 3x + 1 + 3x + 8$

Simplifying Expressions

1. $2 - 1(8x - 3)$

2. $6 + 9x + 2 + 8x$

3. $2 + x - 3 + 7x$

4. $9 + x - 1 + 3x$

5. $-4x - 3 + 8x$

6. $-1 - 4x + 8 - 8x$

7. $-3x + 3x$

Simplifying Expressions

1. $-4x - x$

2. $9x + 1 - 7x + 4 + 2x + 9$

3. $9x - 3x + 9x - 5 + 6$

4. $5 - 7(-7x + 9)$

5. $4x - 8x + x - 8 + 9$

6. $5x + 5 - 7x - 4 + 6x - 1$

7. $-6x - 1 - 8 - 3x$

Simplifying Expressions

① 2x - 1 - 6x + 7

② -x + 7x

③ -2x + 4 + 7x + 3 + 6x - 3

④ -3x + 4 - 6 + 6x

⑤ -5x + 4 + x

⑥ 1 - 3(-3x + 3)

⑦ -9x + 4 - 2x

Simplifying Expressions

1. $1 + 9(3x + 4)$

2. $-9x + 5 - 7 + 8x$

3. $8 - 1(-4x + 1)$

4. $5 + 3(5x - 6)$

5. $5x - 9 - x + 7$

6. $9x - 7x + 9 + 6$

7. $4x + 5 + x$

Simplifying Expressions

(1) $9x - 1 - 7x + 4$

(2) $-5x - 7x$

(3) $-6 - x + 1 - 4x$

(4) $-6 - 9x + 2x - 4 + 4x$

(5) $-6x - 2 + 3x$

(6) $5x - 2 - 5x + 1$

(7) $4x + x$

Simplifying Expressions

(1) $6 - x + 9 - 6x + 6 - 2x$

(2) $x + x$

(3) $8x + x$

(4) $8 + 5x + 5 + 3x$

(5) $-x + 4 - 5x$

(6) $8x + 7 - 4 - 2x + 9x$

(7) $6x - 4x + 3x - 2 + 1$

ANSWERS

Page 1: **Order of Operations (PEDMAS)**

1. **70**   2. **-14**   3. **722**   4. **110**   5. **2,328**   6. **704**

7. **7,810**   8. **-97**   9. **5,776**   10. **1,469**

Page 2: **Order of Operations (PEDMAS)**

1. **82**   2. **246**   3. **608**   4. **9,661**   5. **64,160,147**

6. **2,204**   7. **61**   8. **22,745**   9. **192**   10. **2.5**

Page 3: **Order of Operations (PEDMAS)**

1. **14**   2. **19**   3. **8,226**   4. **-179**   5. **6,390**   6. **54,352**

7. **47**   8. **731**   9. **3,320**   10. **3,526**

Page 4: **Order of Operations (PEDMAS)**

1. **5,690**   2. **2,687**   3. **174**   4. **7,493**   5. **1,455**

6. **-39**   7. **122**   8. **15,681,659**   9. **34**   10. **1,028**

Page 5: **Order of Operations (PEDMAS)**

1. **2,183**   2. **1,147**   3. **-2**   4. **-77**   5. **3,764**   6. **99**   7. **106**

8. **162**   9. **2,098**   10. **1.2**

Page 6: **Order of Operations (PEDMAS)**

1. **12,636**   2. **871**   3. **54**   4. **66**   5. **162**   6. **4,969**

7. **7,810**   8. **2,004**   9. **132**   10. **-48**

Page 7: **Order of Operations (PEDMAS)**

1. **101**   2. **23**   3. **6,545**   4. **-1,107**   5. **1,680**   6. **-179**

7. **13,429**   8. **12,083**   9. **70**   10. **207**

Page 8: **Order of Operations (PEDMAS)**

1. **107**   2. **183**   3. **89**   4. **784**   5. **102**   6. **95**   7. **1.3**

8. **103**   9. **5,364**   10. **176**

Page 9: **Order of Operations (PEDMAS)**

1. **4,144**   2. **300**   3. **4.3**   4. **-95**   5. **-242**   6. **-10**

7. **39**   8. **-252**   9. **10,344**   10. **6,344**

Page 10: Order of Operations (PEDMAS)

1. **-35**   2. **115**   3. **363**   4. **-5,940**   5. **1,386**   6. **-193**

7. **29,354**   8. **-51**   9. **-64**   10. **95**

Page 11: Lowest Common Multiple

1. **30**   2. **60**   3. **33**   4. **40**   5. **90**   6. **84**   7. **99**   8. **77**

Page 12: Lowest Common Multiple

1. **110**   2. **110**   3. **10**   4. **132**   5. **63**   6. **24**   7. **60**   8. **44**

Page 13: Lowest Common Multiple

1. **18**   2. **132**   3. **12**   4. **10**   5. **10**   6. **88**   7. **20**   8. **60**

Page 14: Lowest Common Multiple

1. **21**   2. **36**   3. **110**   4. **10**   5. **60**   6. **60**   7. **77**   8. **12**

Page 15: Lowest Common Multiple

1. **20**   2. **60**   3. **35**   4. **132**   5. **60**   6. **21**   7. **84**   8. **30**

Page 16: Lowest Common Multiple

1. **40**   2. **14**   3. **132**   4. **10**   5. **8**   6. **9**   7. **22**   8. **36**

Page 17: Lowest Common Multiple

1. **24**   2. **132**   3. **30**   4. **60**   5. **66**   6. **30**   7. **10**   8. **18**

Page 18: Lowest Common Multiple

1. **132**   2. **110**   3. **10**   4. **10**   5. **36**   6. **33**   7. **60**   8. **77**

Page 19: Lowest Common Multiple

1. **33**   2. **12**   3. **40**   4. **88**   5. **22**   6. **12**   7. **77**   8. **60**

Page 20: Lowest Common Multiple

1. **66**   2. **14**   3. **110**   4. **9**   5. **28**   6. **36**   7. **24**   8. **60**

Page 21: Fractions: Multiple Operations

1. **1/15**   2. **1 7/20**   3. **10 1/12**   4. **1 7/15**   5. **11/15**

Page 22: Fractions: Multiple Operations

1. **43/72**   2. **1/8**   3. **5/36**   4. **-3/64**   5. **6 1/8**

Page 23: Fractions: Multiple Operations

1. **2 1/3**   2. **13/32**   3. **1/18**   4. **1/6**   5. **35/96**

Page 24: **Fractions: Multiple Operations**
1. **3 11/24**   2. **1**   3. **1 5/24**   4. **3/4**   5. **1/15**

Page 25: **Fractions: Multiple Operations**
1. **63/64**   2. **2/9**   3. **1/5**   4. **8/45**   5. **1/3**

Page 26: **Fractions: Multiple Operations**
1. **41/48**   2. **8 11/12**   3. **85/144**   4. **1/30**   5. **3 9/20**

Page 27: **Fractions: Multiple Operations**
1. **7/24**   2. **7/36**   3. **2/45**   4. **25/48**   5. **73/96**

Page 28: **Fractions: Multiple Operations**
1. **9 5/12**   2. **62/75**   3. **139/180**   4. **301/360**   5. **1/27**

Page 29: **Fractions: Multiple Operations**
1. **1/10**   2. **5/8**   3. **17/24**   4. **1 7/45**   5. **1/3**

Page 30: **Fractions: Multiple Operations**
1. **9 1/12**   2. **2 3/40**   3. **2/75**   4. **17/72**   5. **5**

Page 31: **Equations (One Step) Addition and Subtraction**
1. x = 8   2. x = 8   3. x = 9   4. x = 8   5. x = 9   6. x = 9   7. x = 2
8. x = 3   9. x = 5   10. x = 9

Page 32: **Equations (One Step) Addition and Subtraction**
1. x = 7   2. x = 6   3. x = 5   4. x = 4   5. x = 8   6. x = 6   7. x = 6
8. x = 3   9. x = 4   10. x = 2

Page 33: **Equations (One Step) Addition and Subtraction**
1. x = 4   2. x = 8   3. x = 3   4. x = 7   5. x = 1   6. x = 4   7. x = 5
8. x = 7   9. x = 5   10. x = 7

Page 34: **Equations (One Step) Addition and Subtraction**
1. x = 1   2. x = 3   3. x = 7   4. x = 9   5. x = 9   6. x = 8   7. x = 5
8. x = 7   9. x = 9   10. x = 9

Page 35: **Equations (One Step) Addition and Subtraction**
1. x = 3   2. x = 9   3. x = 8   4. x = 3   5. x = 6   6. x = 1   7. x = 9
8. x = 5   9. x = 7   10. x = 5

Page 36:   Equations (One Step) Addition and Subtraction

1. x = 3   2. x = 3   3. x = 5   4. x = 4   5. x = 6   6. x = 7   7. x = 9

8. x = 1   9. x = 4   10. x = 5

Page 37:   Equations (One Step) Addition and Subtraction

1. x = 3   2. x = 9   3. x = 3   4. x = 4   5. x = 3   6. x = 9   7. x = 6

8. x = 8   9. x = 1   10. x = 7

Page 38:   Equations (One Step) Addition and Subtraction

1. x = 4   2. x = 5   3. x = 3   4. x = 5   5. x = 1   6. x = 6   7. x = 8

8. x = 2   9. x = 6   10. x = 9

Page 39:   Equations (One Step) Addition and Subtraction

1. x = 7   2. x = 1   3. x = 9   4. x = 7   5. x = 7   6. x = 2   7. x = 4

8. x = 3   9. x = 5   10. x = 7

Page 40:   Equations (One Step) Addition and Subtraction

1. x = 4   2. x = 2   3. x = 6   4. x = 2   5. x = 2   6. x = 7   7. x = 9

8. x = 6   9. x = 9   10. x = 2

Page 41:   Equations (One Step) Multiplication and Division

1. x = 9   2. x = 7   3. x = 8   4. x = 3   5. x = 3   6. x = 1   7. x = 56

8. x = 9   9. x = 5   10. x = 7

Page 42:   Equations (One Step) Multiplication and Division

1. x = 8   2. x = 9   3. x = 5   4. x = 1   5. x = 9   6. x = 20   7. x = 3

8. x = 5   9. x = 5   10. x = 8

Page 43:   Equations (One Step) Multiplication and Division

1. x = 6   2. x = 72   3. x = 8   4. x = 6   5. x = 2   6. x = 1   7. x = 5

8. x = 2   9. x = 4   10. x = 4

Page 44:   Equations (One Step) Multiplication and Division

1. x = 5   2. x = 2   3. x = 3   4. x = 9   5. x = 3   6. x = 7   7. x = 5

8. x = 3   9. x = 6   10. x = 8

Page 45:   Equations (One Step) Multiplication and Division

1. x = 9   2. x = 1   3. x = 8   4. x = 3   5. x = 2   6. x = 4   7. x = 8

8. x = 3   9. x = 9   10. x = 8

Page 46:   Equations (One Step) Multiplication and Division

1. x = 9   2. x = 5   3. x = 21   4. x = 7   5. x = 2   6. x = 9   7. x = 9

8. x = 7   9. x = 5   10. x = 8

Page 47:   Equations (One Step) Multiplication and Division

1. x = 6   2. x = 4   3. x = 12   4. x = 40   5. x = 1   6. x = 6   7. x = 9

8. x = 8   9. x = 4   10. x = 8

Page 48:   Equations (One Step) Multiplication and Division

1. x = 5   2. x = 8   3. x = 1   4. x = 5   5. x = 1   6. x = 7   7. x = 3

8. x = 40   9. x = 9   10. x = 1

Page 49:   Equations (One Step) Multiplication and Division

1. x = 1   2. x = 4   3. x = 3   4. x = 4   5. x = 3   6. x = 3   7. x = 6

8. x = 8   9. x = 5   10. x = 5

Page 50:   Equations (One Step) Multiplication and Division

1. x = 9   2. x = 3   3. x = 4   4. x = 1   5. x = 4   6. x = 2   7. x = 4

8. x = 6   9. x = 6   10. x = 4

Page 51:   Inequalities - Addition and Subtraction

1. x > 13   2. x > 7   3. x > -3   4. x ≥ -1   5. x ≥ 2   6. x < -4

Page 52:   Inequalities - Addition and Subtraction

1. x ≤ -1   2. x ≥ 15   3. x < 0   4. x ≥ -2   5. x > -3   6. x < -8

Page 53:   Inequalities - Addition and Subtraction

1. x ≤ -3   2. x ≤ 11   3. x < -2   4. x > 0   5. x > -2   6. x ≥ 6

Page 54:   Inequalities - Addition and Subtraction

1. x ≤ -4   2. x < 7   3. x > 10   4. x ≤ 2   5. x ≤ 0   6. x < 16

Page 55:   Inequalities - Addition and Subtraction

1. x ≤ 3   2. x ≤ 7   3. x > 3   4. x ≤ -2   5. x > -1   6. x ≤ -3

Page 56:   Inequalities - Addition and Subtraction

1. x < 2   2. x > 15   3. x > -6   4. x ≥ -1   5. x < 11   6. x > -2

Page 57: Inequalities - Addition and Subtraction

1. $x > 15$ 2. $x > -5$ 3. $x \leq -1$ 4. $x \leq 6$ 5. $x \leq 9$ 6. $x > 1$

Page 58: Inequalities - Addition and Subtraction

1. $x > 5$ 2. $x < -3$ 3. $x > 17$ 4. $x < -3$ 5. $x < 0$ 6. $x < -6$

Page 59: Inequalities - Addition and Subtraction

1. $x < -5$ 2. $x \leq 4$ 3. $x \geq 17$ 4. $x < 5$ 5. $x \leq -5$ 6. $x \leq -3$

Page 60: Inequalities - Addition and Subtraction

1. $x > -4$ 2. $x \geq 1$ 3. $x < 15$ 4. $x \leq -7$ 5. $x < 3$ 6. $x \geq -3$

Page 61: Inequalities - Multiplication and Division

1. $x \leq 28$ 2. $x > 1/2$ 3. $x > 3/2$ 4. $x \geq 49$ 5. $x \geq 3/2$ 6. $x > 24$

Page 62: Inequalities - Multiplication and Division

1. $x \geq 4/3$ 2. $x > 10$ 3. $x > 1$ 4. $x > 2/3$ 5. $x \leq 28$ 6. $x > 2$

Page 63: Inequalities - Multiplication and Division

1. $x > 8$ 2. $x \leq 5/2$ 3. $x > 4$ 4. $x \geq 5/2$ 5. $x < 2$ 6. $x < 12$

Page 64: Inequalities - Multiplication and Division

1. $x \leq 24$ 2. $x > 3/2$ 3. $x \geq 64$ 4. $x < 1/2$ 5. $x < 6/5$ 6. $x \leq 48$

Page 65: Inequalities - Multiplication and Division

1. $x > 36$ 2. $x < 1/3$ 3. $x < 40$ 4. $x \leq 5/2$ 5. $x \geq 14$ 6. $x \leq 3/2$

Page 66: Inequalities - Multiplication and Division

1. $x < 3/2$ 2. $x \geq 24$ 3. $x > 6/5$ 4. $x \leq 35$ 5. $x < 5/6$ 6. $x < 6$

Page 67: Inequalities - Multiplication and Division

1. $x \leq 16$ 2. $x < 6/5$ 3. $x \geq 6/5$ 4. $x < 8$ 5. $x \geq 12$ 6. $x \leq 2$

Page 68: Inequalities - Multiplication and Division

1. $x < 4/5$ 2. $x \leq 24$ 3. $x \leq 42$ 4. $x < 5/2$ 5. $x \leq 3/4$ 6. $x \geq 12$

Page 69: Inequalities - Multiplication and Division

1. $x \geq 2/3$ 2. $x < 6$ 3. $x > 6/5$ 4. $x > 7$ 5. $x \leq 9$ 6. $x > 5/3$

Page 70: Inequalities - Multiplication and Division

1. $x \leq 2$ 2. $x \geq 36$ 3. $x > 4$ 4. $x > 1$ 5. $x > 3/2$ 6. $x > 25$

Page 71: Pre-Algebra Equations (Two Sides)

1. $x = 4$ 2. $x = 6$ 3. $x = 5$ 4. $x = 6$ 5. $x = 7$ 6. $x = 4$ 7. $x = 8$

8. **x = 5**   9. **x = 6**   10. **x = 6**

Page 72:   Pre-Algebra Equations (Two Sides)

1. **x = 3**   2. **x = 3**   3. **x = 2**   4. **x = 8**   5. **x = 9**   6. **x = 6**   7. **x = 2**

8. **x = 5**   9. **x = 5**   10. **x = 3**

Page 73:   Pre-Algebra Equations (Two Sides)

1. **x = 7**   2. **x = 4**   3. **x = 9**   4. **x = 2**   5. **x = 5**   6. **x = 5**   7. **x = 2**

8. **x = 4**   9. **x = 7**   10. **x = 3**

Page 74:   Pre-Algebra Equations (Two Sides)

1. **x = 5**   2. **x = 4**   3. **x = 7**   4. **x = 7**   5. **x = 4**   6. **x = 7**   7. **x = 8**

8. **x = 5**   9. **x = 9**   10. **x = 6**

Page 75:   Pre-Algebra Equations (Two Sides)

1. **x = 8**   2. **x = 8**   3. **x = 5**   4. **x = 4**   5. **x = 5**   6. **x = 5**   7. **x = 7**

8. **x = 7**   9. **x = 8**   10. **x = 8**

Page 76:   Pre-Algebra Equations (Two Sides)

1. **x = 5**   2. **x = 7**   3. **x = 6**   4. **x = 4**   5. **x = 9**   6. **x = 5**   7. **x = 6**

8. **x = 9**   9. **x = 5**   10. **x = 9**

Page 77:   Pre-Algebra Equations (Two Sides)

1. **x = 5**   2. **x = 4**   3. **x = 7**   4. **x = 5**   5. **x = 2**   6. **x = 6**   7. **x = 4**

8. **x = 3**   9. **x = 2**   10. **x = 2**

Page 78:   Pre-Algebra Equations (Two Sides)

1. **x = 7**   2. **x = 3**   3. **x = 5**   4. **x = 7**   5. **x = 8**   6. **x = 3**   7. **x = 3**

8. **x = 8**   9. **x = 2**   10. **x = 6**

Page 79:   Pre-Algebra Equations (Two Sides)

1. **x = 8**   2. **x = 8**   3. **x = 4**   4. **x = 5**   5. **x = 3**   6. **x = 7**   7. **x = 3**

8. **x = 5**   9. **x = 6**   10. **x = 7**

Page 80:   Pre-Algebra Equations (Two Sides)

1. **x = 7**   2. **x = 6**   3. **x = 7**   4. **x = 4**   5. **x = 5**   6. **x = 9**   7. **x = 7**

8. **x = 2**   9. **x = 4**   10. **x = 8**

Page 81:   Pre-Algebra Equations (Two Sides)

1. **x = 7**   2. **x = 6**   3. **x = 4**   4. **x = 3**   5. **x = 7**   6. **x = 8**   7. **x = 5**

8. **x = 7**   9. **x = 3**   10. **x = 3**

Page 82:   Pre-Algebra Equations (Two Sides)

1. **x = 5**   2. **x = 4**   3. **x = 4**   4. **x = 3**   5. **x = 5**   6. **x = 7**   7. **x = 2**

8. **x = 5**   9. **x = 7**   10. **x = 2**

Page 83:   Pre-Algebra Equations (Two Sides)

1. **x = 8**   2. **x = 9**   3. **x = 9**   4. **x = 5**   5. **x = 6**   6. **x = 2**   7. **x = 8**

8. **x = 4**   9. **x = 7**   10. **x = 7**

Page 84:   Pre-Algebra Equations (Two Sides)

1. **x = 4**   2. **x = 8**   3. **x = 7**   4. **x = 7**   5. **x = 2**   6. **x = 3**   7. **x = 4**

8. **x = 4**   9. **x = 9**   10. **x = 2**

Page 85:   Pre-Algebra Equations (Two Sides)

1. **x = 4**   2. **x = 2**   3. **x = 7**   4. **x = 2**   5. **x = 4**   6. **x = 9**   7. **x = 6**

8. **x = 6**   9. **x = 5**   10. **x = 2**

Page 86:   Simplifying Expressions

1. **2x + 6**   2. **5x + 7**   3. **13x + 4**   4. **2x – 8**   5. **–9x**   6. **–2x – 2**

7. **–6x**

Page 87:   Simplifying Expressions

1. **13x – 7**   2. **x – 4**   3. **–2x + 2**   4. **3x + 2**   5. **–2x + 2**   6. **2x**

7. **9**

Page 88:   Simplifying Expressions

1. **11x + 8**   2. **4x + 1**   3. **2x**   4. **9x + 1**   5. **13x + 8**

6. **5x + 12**   7. **14x – 16**

Page 89:   Simplifying Expressions

1. **3x + 6**   2. **3x**   3. **–5x + 10**   4. **–14x + 11**   5. **–x + 8**

6. **13x – 2**   7. **7x + 10**

Page 90:   Simplifying Expressions

1. **–8x + 5**   2. **17x + 8**   3. **8x – 1**   4. **4x + 8**   5. **4x – 3**

6. **−12x + 7**   7. **0**

Page 91: Simplifying Expressions

1. **−5x**   2. **4x + 14**   3. **15x + 1**   4. **49x − 58**   5. **−3x + 1**

6. **4x**   7. **−9x − 9**

Page 92: Simplifying Expressions

1. **−4x + 6**   2. **6x**   3. **11x + 4**   4. **3x − 2**   5. **−4x + 4**

6. **9x − 8**   7. **−11x + 4**

Page 93: Simplifying Expressions

1. **27x + 37**   2. **−x − 2**   3. **4x + 7**   4. **15x − 13**   5. **4x − 2**

6. **2x + 15**   7. **5x + 5**

Page 94: Simplifying Expressions

1. **2x + 3**   2. **−12x**   3. **−5x − 5**   4. **−3x − 10**   5. **−3x − 2**

6. **-1**   7. **5x**

Page 95: Simplifying Expressions

1. **−9x + 21**   2. **2x**   3. **9x**   4. **8x + 13**   5. **−6x + 4**

6. **15x + 3**   7. **5x − 1**

Daily Math Practice
180 DAYS OF WORKBOOKS
GRADE 1
With Answer Key
KIDS EDU Mentor

Daily Math Practice
180 DAYS OF WORKBOOKS
GRADE 2
With Answer Key
KIDS EDU Mentor

Daily Math Practice
180 DAYS OF WORKBOOKS
GRADE 3
With Answer Key
KIDS EDU Mentor

Daily Math Practice
180 DAYS OF WORKBOOKS
GRADE 4
With Answer Key
KIDS EDU Mentor

Daily Math Practice
180 DAYS OF WORKBOOKS
GRADE 5
With Answer Key
$2 + 2 = 4$
Kids EDU Mentor

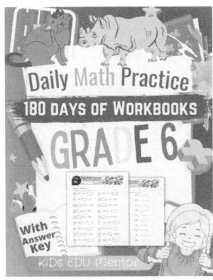

Daily Math Practice
180 DAYS OF WORKBOOKS
GRADE 6
With Answer Key
KIDs EDU Mentor

Daily Math Practice
Pre-Algebra
Grade 6
with answers

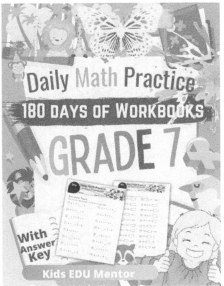

Daily Math Practice
180 DAYS OF WORKBOOKS
GRADE 7
With Answer Key
Kids EDU Mentor

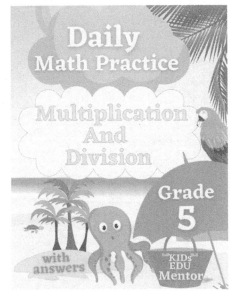

Daily Math Practice
Multiplication And Division
Grade 5
with answers
KIDS EDU Mentor

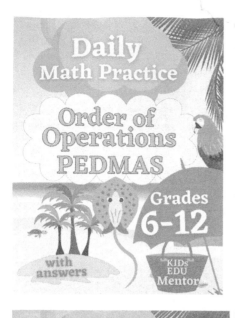

Daily Math Practice

Order of Operations PEDMAS

Grades 6-12

with answers

KIDs EDU Mentor

Daily Math Practice

Pre-Algebra

Grade 7-8

with answers

KIDs EDU Mentor

Daily Math Practice

Multiplication

Grade 5

with answers

KIDs EDU Mentor

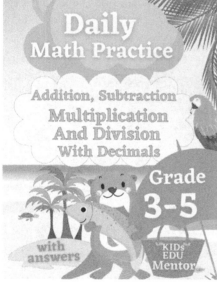

Daily Math Practice

Addition, Subtraction Multiplication And Division With Decimals

Grade 3-5

with answers

KIDs EDU Mentor

Daily Math Practice

Multiplication And Division

Grade 4

with answers

KIDs EDU Mentor

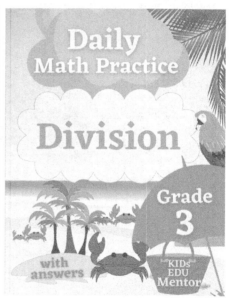

Daily Math Practice

Division

Grade 3

with answers

KIDs EDU Mentor

Daily Math Practice

Fractions

Grade 5

with answers

KIDs EDU Mentor

Daily Math Practice

Multiplication And Division

Grade 3

with answers

KIDs EDU Mentor

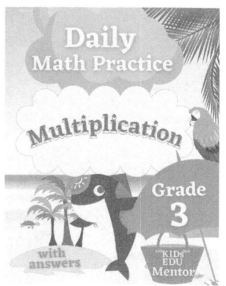

Daily Math Practice

Multiplication

Grade 3

with answers

KIDs EDU Mentor

Made in the USA
Coppell, TX
09 June 2022

78669665R00063